More Sentimental Slop & Haiku

More Sentimental Slop & Haiku by MT (Matthew Thomas) Stolte

Copyright © 2025

ISBN: 978-1-7353850-5-1

First Edition

eMTeVisPub

https://www.lulu.com/spotlight/emtevispub

for Leonard William Stolte

Contents

Part 1 – Senti-

Mom & Dad   2

My 1st Anxiety Attack   7

Ham Sandwiches   8

Peculiar Life   9

Owen Gromme   11

6th   12

The Shadow   15

Fighting with My Little Brother   16

The Quick Red Bike   18

Senior Year Big Guy   20

The Hat   21

The Inn   22

Bad Shit   23

Punks   26

Living in Downtown Portage 1994-
           95   33

Eugene   35

Flute   36

When I Was a Kid …   39

Washing Trucks   42

The Foreman at Lunch	46
Brad	47
The Fishermen at Table No. 5	52
The Hike	55
The Man with Tubes Up His Nose	59

Part 2 – mental

Mania Poem	61
The Pedestal	63
AG & I Die	64
Aunt Carrie	66
Visiting Aunt Carrie	67
Psychiatry	69
The Little Girl	71
Whisky & Free Popcorn	72
The Artist	75
A Week in Jail	78
Things Nadine Said	86
Nadine is Dead Song	87
Red	88
At the Reading	92
The French Busker	93

The Drug Dealer	95
Table for One	96
Van Gogh Before Plastic	98
Portrait of Chris Cornell	99

Part 3 – Slop

All of Creation	101
Without Wine Parts 2-4	102
Market Day Song	108
Pain & Death Song	109
Fart Poem	110
Scene from a Birthday	112
Golden-crowned Kinglet	114
Morning Cooper's Hawk	115
The Eastern Parson Spider	116
The Old Man with the Cane	117
Without Much Money …	119
6 Commercials	120
Portrait of Ron Czerwien	121
White Poetry Chicks	122
Boots	123
Visiting Dad in the ICU	124

Visiting Dad in the ICU the Day

After His Accident the Day Before His Death	126
Eyes Closed Repose	127
Thumbs & Plum	128
Sure	129
The 12 WI Months	130
Eken Park, May 2024	131
Part 4 – Haiku	136
Notes	140

Senti-

Mom & Dad

I was born in 19
73. My parents
were both
18.

We lived on a hill
in Northern South Central
Wisconsin
in a red brick house.
A field before us
leading to a woods; Amy Pond
to the far right
of the fields. A field of grass
and a row of pines
on one side
of us; the farmer
of the fields
on the
other. Behind
was woods, then
swamp, then
man-made Lake
Mason. Dad
worked in tool & dye; Mom
worked at home. I think they both
sold
pot.

I remember many people
over. Smoke &
talk & laugh-

ter. Long scissors with a flat
nose, an old-fashioned Coke tray
with herb on it, plastic
bags & clips &
things. I remember the plain
bong
in the liquor cabinet
the smell of those multi-shaped
hanging glasses, candles & cards
in the upper
drawer. 2 fat square door
handles
& a key hole. Green
felt. Dark
waxy
wood.

We ate vegetarian until
we were all in
school: tofu, bam-
boo, rice, homemade veggie burgers
homemade big bread – hot
out of the oven
with immediate peanut
butter; a terror
at lunch – the jelly'd
seep through like
bruises. A little too
heavy
too.

I remember being home with
Mom. She was young &
always working: dishes, laundry, ex-
ercising, in the garden, preparing

food, canning, making
bread. Soaps on.

Dad came home in dark dirty
jeans. A dark green shirt
or a dark blue
one. He
smelled. He had long black
hair, a big dark gray plastic lunch
box, after the chipped black
metal one. Beaten boots
with sharp, silver, twisted metal bits
stuck in the rubber
soles. He'd mow the lawn
on his day
off (sometimes in a white t-shirt
with the flag on it, bandana
& cut-offs); he'd
work in the
garden. In the fall
we all cut
wood. Winter: shovel.
Double most everything
down at
Grandma's.

I remember the Daisy Duck topless poster
above the
piano (as my friends did). Crumb's
A Short History of America.
The old woman
with paraphernalia in her
lap. Fritz the Cat comics. The
vandalized police man
on the Monopoly board marked

FUZZ. Rolling
Stone, the **Whole Earth
Catalog**, Carl
Sagan, David
Attenborough, Lennon
vinyl
with the spinning
apple, **Big Science
SWEET DREAMS
(are made of this)
Ralf & Florian**
Doctor Who, houseplants
cats &
always at least one
dog. Cranes calling
from the field, Canadian geese
honking overhead, deer
everywhere. Owls, hawks &
snapping turtles.

A long
gravel driveway.

One time
Mom flung a spatula directly into my
face, on accident
as I played airplane on 2 couch
cushions. Dad
would sometimes
yell.

3
kids. 16 years
together. 18 years
in tool &

dye.

1st went the
drugs, then the
vegetarianism, the
marriage, moms, job &
kids.

Decades 6 miles
apart.

My 1st Anxiety Attack

Once
when I was a little guy
I took a bath.
When I was done
I discovered
the living room was full of people
& I had to walk through them
to get to my
clothes in my
room.

"Don't worry," my grandma said.
"Just put that towel around you
& walk through there like a cowboy."

I don't remember
walking through.
That must've been
cute.

I only remember
what my grandma
said.

Ham Sandwiches

One of the best sandwiches I ever had
was a ham sandwich.
Dad brought dozens of them home
in a clear plastic bag
from Grandpa's funeral.

Butter on a white bun
with ham.

Peculiar Life

They lived in a trailer
on a big lot
in an unincorporated village
downtown.

Grandma'd buy soda – whatever we liked.
We liked the new Mandarin Orange Slice
but we'd drink up her Diet 7 Up
too.
White bread, Kraft spread (that'd brown with age)
American cheese slices & lunch meat,
Oscar Mayer variety pack, on a paper plate.

We'd watch late night television
hate the car commercials
fall asleep one by one
go to bed.

In the morning dark
coffee percolated.
A light
& slow slipper steps.
Cornflakes in a shallow, white bowl with sugar.
We'd wake
put the bed up – open the curtains
& eat bacon, scrambled microwave eggs
toast with peanut butter.
For lunch – SpaghettiOs in a saucepan
with melted American cheese
or sandwiches, can ravioli, Kraft macaroni & cheese
or if we're lucky – sloppy joes.

All the Oreos – in a friar monk cookie jar
& potato chips we could down
& we could down a lot. Twinkies in the drawer
doughnuts, chocolates, ice cream
Dreamsicles, popsicles, ice cream sandwiches
Push-Ups.

We'd play outside
look at the bunnies
the teetering windmill, the antenna we'd climb
the tank we'd clang
with a plastic bat or stick or rock
ride it
get white on our pants.

They'd be inside the picture windows
watching Wheel of Fortune
Lawrence Welk, the local news
again & again
Hee Haw, Knight Rider
sports
all
day.

Great-Grandma
from England
kept a hand
against her cheek
eyes bulging endlessly
deaf

she was a skinny thing.

Owen Gromme

Grandma
lived a couple of blocks
down from Owen Gromme's
place. She said
he was an ornery
old man.

We rode our dirt bikes
off the Hwy 23 bridge
into Nina Creek
where snowy egrets would visit
some years
& Gromme painted them.
Walking through the dense marsh
we were afraid
to walk into one.

There was always a painter
in my mind.

6th

I went to country schools (besides
kindergarten)
through 6th
grade.

All I thought about
was the work
put to me &
life around me.

When my parents
took me to buy
new pants
I saw some black
pants
& I bought
several
wearing
hand me down plaid flannels
& sweaters grandmas
bought me.

I don't think I even knew
hair grew down
there
until
hair grew down there.

I ran muddy
football &
we built

forts
out of grass &
garbage.

I had some toys
& gave them to other kids to play
while Neil & I
explored imaginary dungeons
with imaginary
bows.

We
jumped off the
swings &
crushed each other in
huge pileups.

We
ran across the
snow, breaking through
to the slush
underneath &
spent the rest of the day
inside
shoes & socks
along the radiators.

One day
all the girls stayed in for
recess

& later
came out
crying.

When the music teachers came
to our school from
junior high, they
preformed a batch
of instruments for us &
let us
pick & play
them. I finally chose
flute (they
wouldn't let me choose sax
too much interest).

Bussed to junior high
it was

"Only faggots play the flute
& who in the hell wears black jeans
nerd?"

Fitting in
was horrible
for all of us

& Linsey
was a traitor.

The Shadow

When I was a kid
a smooth, black figure haunted my dreams.
Its hand stuck out
from underneath a stall
in my 2nd grade bathroom
as I pissed.
It
followed me down the hill
in the night – it was darker
than the sky.

I decided I'd had enough.
In a dream
I followed it, walked through the house
towards it.

When I found it
it was
one of the guys
from Monty Python
dressed in pink like
one of the guys
from the Sgt. Pepper
album

& it was
laughing, laughing
& laughing.

Fighting with My Little Brother

My brother & I
fought passionately – I
don't know how it got so
violent.

One day
we were throwing aluminum
badminton rackets
at each other from a distance
on the back side
of the hill
by a stand of red
pine &
the sewer.

I hit him in the face – the racket
took the shape of his
profile
& split his nose.
He was rushed to the clinic
as I crouched between
the 2 big pines
at the top of the hill
condemned by
my own
negativity.

We stopped fighting
after that
though
the last time we wrestled with Dad

he squashed my balls.

The Quick Red Bike

My dad
bought a big red
Schwinn; my mom
got a red
Panasonic.
Rarely did they
bike
together – we
never
all
went.

Summer. I was
15. I got up
around 4:30
6 days a week
& got picked up.
A man, his boy
(later his boys)
in his turquoise Chevette
with faux wood grain
across the doors & rust –
I had many duties.
My dad drove away
later.

Mom
rode her quick red
10-speed – bandanna & shorts
5 miles through the woods
the deer

the sun, cloud, blue & wind
up hills, down hills
sweat & puff & cruise
foreign corn & house & farm

to Loren's.

Senior Year Big Guy

He wasn't really a bully
but he was BIG –
he flipped a tall, geeky student
over in the hallway –
the geek had a seizure
flapping on the tile in the crowd
like an upside-down electric toy.

In math class he said,
"A woman raping a man
is like trying to stick a sponge
into a Coke bottle."

The Hat

I found
a pretty cool hat
in the lost & found box
at work.
I wore it that evening
to a restaurant
where I sat around
drinking tea.

On my way out
alone, a large group of men
shouted at me.
One man screamed

"Hey!
How much do you want for that hat?"

"$20," I said
&
he got his hat.

The Inn

I made beds
with a woman
whose best friend
had been
Jesus
then later
the Devil.

It turned out
fine – she
started her own
church.

I quit.

Bad Shit

I was with Max
& his friend.
We pulled up to some apartments
on the far east side
of Madison
in Max's purple
beast.

We smoked
then went in.

There was a narrow entrance
which opened into the kitchen.
In the next room
the living room
a large group of kids
our age
were huddled
on & around a couch
staring at a
television.
One guy
had a snake
around his
neck.

I turned back
to the kitchen.
Some man mentioned a beer
& my eyes went
black.

I was blind
so I slumped down
to the
floor.
2 faint, white, female outlines
moved in the blackness
& they were saying

"Are you tripping?"

"No," I said
not mentioning
that I was
blind.

I sat there
awhile
considering
being
blind
for
life.

My vision
suddenly came
back – I was sitting
in a used, pizza delivery
box. I moved towards the door
where
coincidentally
Max & his friend
had gathered.

We got in the car
& asked each other

what happened. They'd gone blind too.
Then we all
passed out
in the
car.

When we came to
Max said

"That must've been bad shit.
My dad asked me
where the hell I got that shit."

Punks

I was alone
in the city of my birth
up-
stairs
down-
town
waiting
for
her.

I was
2
2
riding
with a guy
3 years younger. He
mostly sold drugs
to pay
his parents
rent. We
raved together. He
was an unlikely
good
friend.

I
had
dropped
out
raving on weekends
waiting

in a Chinese restaurant
&
reading.

We drove around a lot. He
introduced me
to some punks he met
from Point
at a rave. I thought
that was cool – I
didn't know any
punks.

They were dealing
acid. We
drove up to
Point. We
disclosed we were neither
gay nor
bi.

They all met
my friend & 3
of them
at my
apartment. The punks
all wore
black – leather, netting.
The leader
was a woman. I
liked her – she was
a lesbian – danced
for a punk
band.

There were 2 guys
I'd never seen before. 1
was demure
in a leather skit. The other
was a little
rascal.

The 4 of them sat in my living
room – delt
the acid
1st thing – Samantha, the leader
ate a
10.

I made a yellow chip bowl
of cherry Kool-
aid – the powder
rose – Max
was drink-
ing. Me
too. I gave the leader
a CD. I played
The Power of Pussy – she said
that was 1 of her favorite records.

I looked a little am-
bivilant. At a party with Max
a fat man doing his 1st
paper
laughed
pointed at me
continuously
shouting, "You look like the Devil!
You're
EVIL!!"

I said I
was.

I had short hair, combed it
down. I wore tight t-
shirts, fat
jeans.

We walked – 2
ravers
3
punks
to a gas station late night convenience store.
Walking
there
we were stopped
by 3 local
cop cars.

5 of us
in line. A
dark complexioned man
with a mustache
walked side to
side
in front of us
& the other 2
cops.

We were held
45
minutes. They
gave us blow
jobs (but
me). The rowdy one

pretended
he couldn't
blow
hard enough. The skirt
guy
told the mustached cop
a story about
the Marines. He
had to jump
out of a plane. The guy
in front of him
didn't pull the
cord
&
bounced so far
from the ground
he almost hit him
parachuting
down.

They had to let us
go
though
Max had been drinking – he
didn't take the B
J because
he said
they had no right to.
I guess they didn't because they
didn't.

They asked me not to put my hands
in my pockets; they told us
we smelled like
pot. "I know what it smells

like," mustache
said.

The truth was
Samantha had a book of acid
on her
person
but she didn't
run.

We walked to the store
walked back
hacked outside a couple bars
under bright white lights
next to a new car lot.

It was all in all
a good night.

One day
there was a knock
on my door. I was
packing for a 3-day
rave up
north.

It was a detective. He said
he had me on video-
tape
trashing cars. I told him
to go the hell
away. He said he knew I hated
the town. I told him I
did. He told me the others
cooperated, my

friends. I told him they weren't my
friends.

He
left.

My girlfriend flew
over. We got married
across the street. I got
a ticket for marijuana possession
coincidentally
from that same detective
a few weeks
later. We (the newlyweds)

drove a few thousand miles
west

a few weeks before
spring.

Living in Downtown Portage, 1994-95

Before I painted
she painted a simple mountain
& one day we worked together
on egg cartons
& hung them up.
We both waited tables
paid $250 for that apartment
in downtown Portage –
The Courthouse (bar)
across the street &
the real courthouse kitty corner.
We
had Tsingtao with take-out
at night.
We
drank wine, smoked pot &
took mushrooms there; we
threw a rave afterhours party
there – kids sitting along the wall
from Iowa
smoking meth.
The guy was there
who ODed
a few years later.
We worked
ate out
had a screwdriver
at The Courthouse occasionally
went biking
went for drives –
she couldn't believe

the amount of snow.

One morning in April
we decided to leave town.
The state.
We called the landlady
packed the car
she took the cash
from the register after
the lunch rush
I had my tips
& we did
that.

Eugene

We
had a bedroom
but there was nothing in it
but clothes in the closet
blankets on the carpet
& us
naked
with a bottle
of cheap champagne.

I worked for $5 an hour
washing trucks; she temped.
Rain all winter no snow –
we'd escaped WI
& CO.

Pine coved buttes, Hendricks Park
the biggest magnolia I'd ever seen
likewise, rhododendron, crocus
CA poppies, daisies
hot in the summer
banana slugs, snails & salamanders
in the damp shade
Steller's jay raucous call from a branch
spotted towhee kicking back dirt
western tanagers darting through pine tops
western scrub-jays guarding sidewalks
looking up at me
soft
gray & blue.

Flute

I became
1st flute
in high
school. I
was the only
male
flutist. When
I was asked
in elementary school
what instrument I wanted to play
I said, "saxophone"
but was told
only a very few people
could choose that
so I chose
flute instead. I had no idea
that choosing the flute was
gay.

The older girls
were upset
that I became
1st flute. They verbally
picked on me. One time
I was nervous
& decided to count
the bars of music
on our next
piece
just out of
curiosity

& after I did
that
2nd or 3rd
flute
gave me
living hell
wildly counting the lines too
smacking the music
mocking me
shouting, "What in the hell
are you counting for?"
I didn't
know. I was counting
because I was nervous.

Before I go to work in the morning
now, 30 years later
I often check the stove
more than
once
& also check
to see if my candles are still
lit. That's
routine. Once in awhile
a burner is
on – a candle
is still
lit. If so
I turn it off – blow it out
& go, lock the door. I never
check the door.
If I ever fail to lock it
let them take everything inside
burn it down
pawn my guitars

computer
whatever else is salable –

like I did with my flute
to pay the rent
when I was a very young
man

2,000 miles
from home.

When I Was a Kid My Classmates & Friends Used My Name Itself as a Putdown

I took the steps
2 x 2
in my black rubber boots.
I looked like happy hell.
It was 9:30 p.m.
The past few hours
passed as dreams pass.
Vic, the resident manager
was leaning on the rail
1st floor up, bent 90°
to it, black & gray & very
baked (it is summer).
I waved
said, "Hey," with a smile.
He replied, "Hey.
Stoltes, Stoltes
Stoltes …"

I went to work at 8 a.m.
& scrubbed & sprayed
drove around in the truck
hooked up
finally now (after years of rest)
to the master blaster – 1st time
for me
joking, fucking around, fucking
with each other, another
new guy, 30 something
pretty cool, full of drugs, work
wife, kid. He said

"I bought a parrot
for my oldest daughter.
Quaw! Quaw!" we laughed.

After 5 p.m. I said
"It's not funny."

The foreman
stopped the wand – "What?"

"It's not funny."

"Well, we've gotta do it."

"Why?"

"You wanna go home, go home,"
he said
15 blocks
from the shop.

"Did I say I wanted to go home?
Of course I don't wanna go home!
C'mon!"

Back at the shop
we said our tender
thanks & goodbyes. I'd
torn a tiny hole
in the crotch
of my thrift store
jeans.

I wore my hole
up the stairs

of my building
& all Vic Alfonso could say
was
"Stoltes Stoltes …" as he stared
over the black, lamp lit
campus.

Washing Trucks

Around
2, I think it was
we went to that
Mart.

Actually
it was a gigantic
lot
surrounded by blank walls, trucks &
trailers. Where there was fence
there were trucks, walls, & lots
beyond a thin strip
of a ditch.

The trucks looked
small
in that
lot. The foreman
would drive 1 to me
& I would wash
it: 1st
roll the ladder to the
front
& scrub the dome
with the long brush. Then down
starting with the tires
& work my way
around.

I was hoping
my wife

would find a good
job.

Then
the truckers
would start coming in.
It was like being surrounded
by velociraptors. Then
it would
rain. We
covered our heads with a cap
stocking cap &
hood. The water'd
rise
flow with the acid & soap
into the grate &
ditch.

In the summer
I scrubbed the bugs
off
from the back of the mirrors, the
bars
& from the
grill; in the winter
the wheels & frame
were covered with thick
mud. I'd brush; he'd
acid & soap
& power spray
away.

She
never
found

that
job, though
we both
worked
several
jobs. We moved to the coast.
Just yesterday
we went to that
Mart
looking for a sweatshirt
for her father
something with Oregon
on it. We asked a man
& he said

"We have nothing from the area
here."

I remember watching the soap run
white
with a curious blue
hue
&
trying
in the rain
to witness the poetry
in
that.

One time
a giant soap bubble
rose from the pickle bucket
& slowly drifted
above the buttes in the distance.

A long yellow hose for the wand
skating the lime green brush heads
to the next
truck.

The Foreman at Lunch

We drove thru Burger King
on Friday – he
collected all the toys
from that movie.

"Stocking stuffers,"
he said
"for my little girl.
She sure wants
the one.
Damn!
They never have that one!
Fuck, man!"

He showed me his little girl's
face. She isn't
his.

Brad

"Brad's on the phone!"

"Fucker!"
I'd yell.

"Hey."

"Hey."

"What's up?"

"Not much.
How about you?"

"Nothin'."

"Yeah?"

"What are you doin'?"

"Ah…"

We
went over there
once.

My wife heated up
wine with
spices;

Brad & I
went out for
a 4-pack of
wine coolers;
Marie &
Brad's girlfriend
talked.

We
got back.
Their kid
fingered a
pastry.

So
Marie & I
drank wine;
they
each had a cooler
on their couch.

When Brad
& I
bought the
4-pack
we also
went into
Blockbuster Video.

I was
laughing. There
were figurines
by the counter.
In fact
there were all sorts

of things
by the
counter –
like a miniature
department store
we were.

I eyed the
Star Wars
guys.

"Hey
imagine
if they made
working class
guys. Like
Doug (the foreman)
you know? Wouldn't
he look cool
with his stocking cap
pulled down
over his cap & his
rain gear on &
the mac 10 wand?
Wouldn't that be
bad ass?"

"Stupid,"
he
laughed.

We watched the tape.
It had HOT parts.
Marie & I
got drunk

on
our
couch.

Visuals of an s/m
sex party. There
was a part
where one person
painted another person's
face – it
was a very
mystical
part.

Doug had said
that he thought
Brad was a member
of some
Spanish
gang bangers – I
thought
he was
black.

One day
Brad was sitting
down
on the chair
by the edge
of the bay.

"Hey.
What's up?"
I asked.

"Nothin'."

"What's
up?"

"I have to find
a new place to live."

"Why?"

"'Cause I can't afford it by my-
SELF!"

"Why?"

"My girlfriend moved out."

"You break up?"

"I GUESS."

I wrote this
because I put in
a CD I'd let him
borrow. Lungfish
Pass & Stow.

"Is this the tape
Mommy & I sing
with you?"

"Yes, Nickolis,"
Brad said.

The Fishermen at Table No. 5

Rain.
40 miles an hour
wind. In from
it. Pitcher of beer
breadsticks
& a pizza with
an impromptu list
of items. 2 fishermen
slouched to
table No.
5.

A man with a belly
& bushy mustache
on the
left; a young man
with baked eyes
& a sharp goatee
on the
right. His eyes
his smile
slit to a
razor. Both wore base-
ball caps; both
were
dirty. The big guy
in a Raiders
coat, was
nice
polite
drunk – eyes

2 sad
sunny-side up.

"It's all good,"
he said
after the young guy
spilled.

A man came in
wearing a yellow rain
jacket, glasses
& a smart
dark
hat.

He had a glass of
Chablis. The fisher-
men got
loud-
er.

An older man
joined the wine
drinker, but
didn't
order anything.

I was standing
in the back of the dining
room. 2 men quiet; 2
men loud &
quiet, loud & then
quiet, like
the wind & the
rain.

They looked out-
side; they
stared at me
slouched.

The young one lit
a smoke. I asked him to
go outside. They
decided to
go. "Hey, ese,"
the young man
said, "You speak Spanish?"

I said
nothing. He spoke
more Spanish.
The other man
was
drunk
too
as he
went
out.

They left the pizza in its box
on the green & white striped plastic
tablecloth
on the table
outside. It
soaked up the storm.

The Hike

We decided
to go
hiking. As I waited
for her
to come down
I stood in front
of an open door. An
old man
I'd been introduced to
sat there. I said
hello – he
didn't
get up.

My wife came down
& also said hello &
he still
didn't
get up. He watched us
go.

It was off
101 – a drive
in the
trees. We
had just begun
up the path with
the brown trunks & green
canopy high
up when
I saw a creature in a ditch. We

stopped &
looked
down. "What
is it?" she
said. "It's
a salamander," I
replied. It
was mud brown like
the mud &
it floated there looking
at us. It
swam toward us our
faces bent
to it & then it
walked step
by
step, head
up.

"Are the poisonous?"
I asked.

"I don't know,"
she said.

It
bit
the air
between us. I
watched; my wife
walked up the trail
a bit. "Come here,"
she said.

I looked at the salamander.

"Come here!
I found a toad
or something."

A frog splashed into
the salamander's
mud puddle.

"Here's one too!"
I shouted.

We walked
heard a shout
as a man on a mountain bike
came down
fast. Then
another. We
walked & periodically
stopped.

We noticed
the thin
trees, the
large
stumps. A
man & woman
in jogging clothes
jogged by. The man said,
"Afternoon."

"Recreation area has a sick
sound to it," I said.

"Isn't it weird

how things
decay?" she
said.

As we walked &
stopped back, the
jogging man & woman
passed us again &
again the man said,
"Afternoon."

When we stopped
to see the salamander
again, it
looked back
& slowly sank
down.

Home
the old guy's door
was closed.

The Man with Tubes Up His Nose

1-room apartment
bed & 2 chairs by the door
microwave next to the television
he had a son that rarely visited.
I never saw anyone visit him.
My wife said
"Don't go visit that old man."
When we split
the old man said
"She wasn't good looking anyway."

He gave me his business card
which simply read, after his name
PROBLEM SOLVER.
He talked about the riots.
He nuked fish with salsa.
He had tubes up his nose
& checkered pants.
He pinched pills from a mayonnaise cap
regularly. I drank
from a 1.5L bottle
of red.
I enjoyed the
simplicity.
I admired it.

I moved.
He died.

Florence OR
1997.

mental

Mania Poem

In the beginning of my mania
      everything ran away from ya.
Bottle cap in the hub cap
      army bag for the roadkill raccoon.
In the beginning of my mania
      everything pertains to ya.
We knew what it was all about
      we were asleep & up & about.
In the beginning of my mania
      rain was manna you betcha bananas
baby carrots thrown at cars
      "Hey, knock it off!"
In the beginning of my mania
      black cloud night swirl above clone city
evil spirits sieved through my heart
      new street pavement sealed the graves.
In the beginning of my mania
      backyard graveyard midnight at noon.
In the heat of my mania
      nothing much is stoppin' ya.
In the heat of my mania
      the rainbow ash leaves melted like American
      cheese.
In the heat of my mania
      grey aliens twisted out of my TV
I was on trial, the court of the government
      aliens, vampires & the mafia.
In the heat of my mania
      creatures discussed & walked amongst us
sci-fi clinic waiting area
      Indian shadow giants up in trees blocking stars.

In the heat of my mania
        4 bike rides a day – look out I'm comin' at cha.
In the heat of my mania
        I lost 25 pounds! I saw the tree come down!
I knew when you left town!
        I wouldn't've let the puppy drown!
In the heat of my mania
        nuthin slips passed ya.
Pajamas & pumas
        pom-poms & pow-wows.
In the beginning of my mania
        heaven, blossom, fall color, shadow
snow boots, ice hearts
        mudpuddle splash stomp
wildflower & funk
        centrifugal gunk.
In the end of my mania
        I realized I'd been inna.
I regret the anger.

The Pedestal

When I was in the mental hospital
I put my bed up on its side
to use as a pedestal
for my poetry books.
A staff team came in
one blocked me from
the others, who put the bed
back down.

"Don't do that,"
they said.

Ever since
I've stood in my rooms
drunk
singing.

AG & I Die

Never flew into such a bummer –
    I get kicked out bars
not countries.

Ginsberg's information hair
    in the sheets.

I left Boulder
    for OR
but couldn't make it
    other side of WY –
too many prescriptions
    drugged
24 years old –
    back page
of The Boulder Weekly
    on the seat read
Allen Ginsberg was reading
    that night! Too late
to make it back –
    The Ballad of the Skeletons.

Allen passed in '97; I
    got caught by
farmers, county cops &
    health care professionals
in humid WI July noon sun
    handcuffed, belly scarred on hood
shins shredded in gravel
    shoulders pressed back out of place
to wake me up!

      Just out of my mind '98
up 7 days
     to die.

Aunt Carrie

When I was thrown into Saint Charles
Mental Health Institute
my 2 aunts
brought me gifts. Aunt Carrie
brought me the following books:

**Holidays in Hell, One Thousand & One
Nights, The Odyssey, The
Pilgrim's Progress** &
Welcome to the Monkey House.

I said, "I'm crazy.
I think I might be Jesus Christ
or something."

She replied, "Maybe you are."

That
helped.

Visiting Aunt Carrie

There was a pool
at her apartment
so I brought my
swimming trunks.
I was on mood stabilizers
& what not
not long out of
the hospital. The water
was bleachy blue.
As I bobbed from where the blue
met the sky
Aunt Carrie talked about the universe
being completely unreal
& something about
Jesus.

Inside the apartment
packed
with boxes & junk
a slim path
leading from one point
to another
boyfriend sitting on the floor
on a beat-up futon mattress
against the wall
smoking a joint & playing a cheap
vintage electric bass without an amp
I couldn't figure out
if the shower curtain
went inside or outside
the tub. I got it

wrong. (When I 1st got out
of the hospital
I couldn't write a complete sentence
until I got off of
lithium.)

After my shower, my aunt
dressed in 2 sweaters in the July heat
wanted to show me something.
She led me into the bedroom.
I sat on the bed
which was surrounded with
clothes & stuff. The sliding
closet doors were open.
The closet was
packed
aside from a little space
in the lower left corner. "See,"
she said, "I built a shelf
to put things on."

This shelf
was about 2' tall
& looked like it could hold
about 6 pairs of
shoes. "Great," I said
then
drove home.

Psychiatry

She asked me
"How much do you drink
when you
drink?"

I found the question
difficult
to answer, thinking – drinking
is a gerund
like
skiing.

I'd crashed my car
over an irrigation ditch
at the lowest speed
the cruise control
would set. She said
that was dangerous. I said
"But I was in the early morning
countryside. What's so
dangerous
about that?"

"A telephone pole?"

I sold my car
in 2004
for environmental reasons
& to learn how to ride
the bus.

& I
count
my drinks
now.

The Little Girl

in the waiting room
stared at me
hitting a drum.

I looked at her
she stared at me

the doctor & Mom
came to get her.

Whisky & Free Popcorn

My Chinese, visiting professor
      of literature
(he specialized in William Faulkner)
      lived in the smallest room
of the 4
      upstairs @ 20 E Gorham St
Madison WI
      (I was in the biggest).
He visited NYC
      & was ecstatic
"Finally, a real American city!"
      He'd been to DC a couple times
& referred to it as a park.

He brought over
a giant plastic jug
of whisky
to celebrate.

I was never much of a
      liquor drinker.
As we sat @ my pub table
      in the window
facing Gorham
      I drank it like water.

"Woah. I've never seen anyone
      in my life
drink as much whisky as you."

"I have a tolerance,"

I said.

When he left
I locked the door
slid the
      chain
& fell flat over backwards
for about 15 hours.

When I woke
it felt like I was
trippin'
& I remembered
I had a job interview
in an
hour.

I drove to the movie theater
sort of hallucinating.
Inside, a man in a suit
took me up the spiral stairs
in the lobby of the old Hilldale theater.
There was like a little room
perched up there
with a desk inside.

"You take tickets, serve concessions
you can stand in the back
      & watch movies for free.
Sometimes we have special events
      you may be asked to attend."

It was Robert Redford's theater.
      Sundance.

"You can have free popcorn."

"How much do you pay?"

"$5 an hour,"
he said
repeating the inclusion of
free movies &
popcorn.

"I can't pay my rent
on $5 an hour,"
I said.

"Then this interview is over,"
he said
closing his folder
abruptly standing
to escort me back down
those metal, black
spiral stairs. I'd

always wondered
about those
stairs.

The Artist

I met him
in his apartment/ studio
during an open studios
event – he lived
a block down.
The event
was slow
for both
of us
on our busy
1-way
street.

He
drank. He
would go into the kitchen
pour another glass
of whisky
sit down & set the glass
on the arm, have a swallow
set it back down
spill it
get up & do it
all again.

He'd
finally pass out
on the floor
for a few minutes
& wake up crying. His
parents were alcoholics. White

wine.

He's
the only person I
knew
who would pass out
in slow motion – he'd
be just inches
from the ground
before he finally
hit.

I was irritated
he introduced me
to a young woman
w/o telling me
she was his ex. He'd
given me
1 of his paintings on paper
sold 1 like it
for $2,000 – I
threw it
away.

I just thought it was funny
how he'd only take 1 sip
of his drink
before knocking it to the floor
& w/o a sound or
change of mood would non-
chalantly
go into the kitchen
come back, have a sip
knock it to the floor
& get up & come back

& ... that's a lot of whisky.
A lot of good whisky.
A lot of good whisky wasted.

Like our art.

A Week in Jail

They changed the law.
Was I even guilty
    the 1st time?
WI changed the BAC
from 1 to 0.08%
in 2003
adding
5 days minimum jail time
for a 2nd OWI in less than
5 years.

I had a year to schedule
my time. I drew
0.09
a few weeks less
than 5 years (I've heard many
0.09 stories).

I kept pushing my scheduled jail time
back
all the way
to the last day
which happened to be the Sunday
after Madison's giant
Halloween party on State Street
Freak Fest 2004.

I reported to jail
@ 6 a.m.
after watching **Star Wars**
eating a stir-fry

that included a few
psychedelic mushrooms –
it was the only time
I was CONVINCED
Darth Vader KNEW
the X-wing pilot was his son
& he let him GO – even
@ the expense of the Death Star
itself.

The relatively small room
was full of sleeping kids along the walls
screaming mothers & fathers
costumes & Halloween accessories.

"Have a seat & someone will be w/ you
shortly," a woman behind a foggy window
said.

I set my little bag of toiletries
on a chair. No one
came.

I sat there for hours. Bored
I went outside
for some fresh air. Back in
I played w/ the costumes
& accessories. I put a noose
around my neck
& was immediately arrested
for attempted suicide. He
was the 1st officer I'd seen all morning.
In handcuffs, in the waiting room
a couple sheriffs appeared
& found my little

bag.

"This guy is *reporting* to jail,"
one of them said.

"Drop the charges."

I was freed of my handcuffs
& dragged to
jail.

"You don't get a mattress
or a pillow,"
the dragger said.

I was put in an observation cell
in maximum security – top floor
behind
3 doors (like a cell in a chamber
beyond an airlock).

"Take off all your clothes."

I did.

"Your glasses too."

"I can't see w/out my glasses,"
I said.

"Take them off."

I took them off
& they gave me a giant green
sleeveless

suicide smock
to wear.

"Can I get my medication?"
I asked.

"We'll see what we can do."

That night
no mattress no pillow no slippers
    (feet get cold in institutions)
I took off my full-length vest
& slept on it
in the giant observation window
under a camera.
I wonder how many hard-ons I had
that night
& the next. A bald inmate
looked in my cell window
eyes widening.
A cinnamon-haired sheriff
sat across from my window
@ a desk all night.
She looked like a
conservative, country music fan.
I had a Brazilian neighbor @ the time
so I thought
what the hell
beats sleeping on concrete.
I sleep naked anyway.

Day 3
a short, shaved head, Buddhist monk
mental health professional
in a maroon & yellow robe

came to my
door.

"Why you want to kill yourself?"
she asked.

My face was pressed against the
porthole glass
'cause I couldn't see.

"I don't WANT to kill myself,"
I said.

"Oh very good!"
she exclaimed
clapping her hands
spinning around
robes twirling
as she exited.

In a minute or 2
I was given my glasses, a blue
jail uniform
& was moved across the room
into a normal
cell. It was smaller, darker
though had a toilet & mattress.
Push-ups
were all I could do
in there. I could hear
but not see
the TV
in the common area
as it was flush
with my outer wall.

We were let out
of our personal cell
once a day for an hour
to shower, walk
change the TV channel.
There were 6 cells in there
a slim shower
& the observation cell.
I was across
from a Haitian guy
who wouldn't
eat.
He was
scared.

There was a white
bipolar guy
next to him. We could talk
from our little
windows.

"I know a little French,"
I said.

"Get him to eat,"
bipolar said.

There was an old cannibal
in the 1st cell
along my side
of the room. He
talk crazy.

A group of police

came in
to get the Haitian to eat.
He wouldn't
so they handcuffed him to his bed
& injected him w/ some
liquid food.

I got his attention
after that.

"You want to go to Mendota,"
(Mental Health Institute)
I said. "It's better there,"
I assured him.

He got out.

It was the 2004 US
presidential election
(I voted absentee).
John Kerry
had just been in town
w/ Bruce Springsteen.
He lost
after confusion in
Ohio. There was a riot
in population. The woman
who let me out
once a day
got hit in the head
by a chair
& didn't let me out
that day.

Around 4 a.m.

the next morning
my cell lights woke me.
A sheriff
came to get me.

"We're letting you out early
because you didn't get let out
of your cell yesterday."

Break of dawn
I felt like George Clooney
in a disheveled tux
walking home
across the capitol
square.

Things Nadine Said

"Join us! Another day
shot to hell."

"See that?"
she said
pointing to a mole on her arm.
"That's cancer."

"That's not how you treat a book!"
she shouted after I flung a volume
to land perfectly
flat. I was offended
momentarily
as an author.

"I'll never stop,"
she said
meaning drinking.

"Stay wet."

Nadine is Dead Song

Nadine is Dead, Nadine is Dead
Beer cans & pills
Sitting at her computer
For Days & Days & Days.

I could be dead too right now
For Days & Days & Days
Unanswered texts, Unanswered calls
Unwritten emails.

When a friend is dead it's like fish'n
You are on the hook
Death casts you out in dark water
Where some fish will bite.

I don't believe in accidents
Why was Nadine all alone?
I'll never cook for her again
Her ashes in an urn.

Red

In the lunchroom
she began condescending
when I told her
I didn't know the actor's name
from Star Trek.
She said
the actor's cat
was on Twitter
& that cats
rule the planet

& that I was foolish
to disbelieve
this.

One of her favorite phrases was
"batshit crazy"
like the senator from
her home state
Michele Bachmann.

Before her IT, long-time boyfriend
dumped her
she described him
as being depressed.
"Like Marvin
from **The Hitchhiker's Guide
to the Galaxy**?"
I suggested.
There was meanness
in her laughter.

She'd
say things to me
under her breath
as we passed each other
in the workplace
like alcoholics do.

She said she only drank
1
when she went out
but I often saw her
unable to
stand
after a night
of drinking.

She made fun of love
& darkness came out of her mouth
early in the a.m.

She liked to dance in clubs
& keep her skin
out of the sun
(& was vitamin D deficient)
always wearing
black
dying her hair
red.

You've seen her.

She liked to flirt
but didn't
fuck.

Our relationship as friends
deteriorated
the 4th month after her breakup.
I didn't want to see
her
& she finally texted
"I don't feel comfortable
being alone with you"
after
meeting every weekend
for the farmers' market
for
years.

She admitted
she was once
strangle fucked
by a friend
until she passed out.
One of her boyfriends
ran over her with his car
mashing a leg up
over her head.
Another ex
committed suicide.

In her younger days
she danced for a club
& stuffed dirty socks
in a man's mouth
to get him off.
She went to
a school for bad girls
& fucked them.

Her white shower curtain
was smeared with
faux blood.

faux blood
faux hair
faux sex
faux men
faux jobs
faux books
faux films
faux food
faux fuck
faux friend

Faux get it.

At the Reading – *for Tony Robinson*

We all read
in the red & blue flashing light.
When I signed-up
I asked
"What's going on?"

"Possible shooting."

I thought to myself
½ drunk
I hope it wasn't another
unarmed, young, African American
man
shot
by a white
officer.

It was.

Willy Street
Madison WI
Friday March 6th
2015

The French Busker

I'd been reading Ray Kurzweil
& thinking about
shit
sitting outside a coffee house.
Only a French busker out there
playing beautiful songs
plucking his
acoustic. He was
dirty.

I asked him about
shit
& told him I was a
poet.

He said
Americans were so stupid
that
he didn't want to hear
my stupid poetry
that
my poetry
was
shit.

Then he played another
beautiful song
stroking the nylon
singing
in falsetto.

I felt like I was in
a Jim Jarmusch movie.

When he finished
he assailed me
a 2nd
time.

I saw him again once
getting on the bus
with his guitar in a gig bag.
He looked
exactly
the same.

He looked
like
shit.

The Drug Dealer

He's been walking around
w/o his shirt on
right down the middle
of the
street. Taking my bike out
of the basement
he was sitting
at the top of the stairs
by my
marigolds, alone. He moved
speaking a language
of his own (street).

"Don't forget your cigarettes," I said.
He nodded repeatedly, mumbling.
His skin didn't look like
meth
that day.

My marigolds
this year
twice as tall
as last
planted along the concrete basement stairwell
orange, red outta the verdure
peace
for poets.

Table for One

She left an opened
      cup of vanilla &
      cup of chocolate
pudding
on the top of the washer
next to an empty plastic bag
& a smear of
red.

How she got into the basement
I don't know.

I'd brought my bike in
from an early spring
post-work-drink-lunch-nap ride
little flowers of all colors
      bright green shoots
           humps of dirty snow
like misplaced rocks.

She sounded normal enough
said she lived there
but on her way
out of the basement
she paused in the doorway
& asked
"Why you gotta weapon?"

"I don't have a weapon."

"In your pocket."

"It's just my phone
& my keys are in my other pocket."

"No, your other pocket."

"What pocket?"

"Behind you."

"I don't have a weapon," I said
raising my voice a little.

She left
& stood in the doorway
of the front door
phone to her
ear
as I pushed water
out of the basement
for a few minutes.

When I went upstairs
I didn't make eye contact
then looked out the fisheye
until she walked away
backpack on
destination
unknown.

Van Gogh Before Plastic

Van Gogh
never got to listen to
Hound Dog Taylor
on vinyl.
Van Gogh
never wore yoga pants.
Van Gogh
didn't have Amazon
to work for
to support his
art
to
purchase
paints.

But he did know
the postman
& wrote many letters
in his starry night
by his flame
letters that became
unbearably
sad.

Portrait of Chris Cornell

After Soundgarden's final show
he hugged everyone in the band.
He'd never done that before.

He was saying goodbye
As the seasons roll on by

Slop

All of Creation

I read today
that in Greek mythology
Eurynome rose out of
Chaos – like
phlegm out of
soup or something &
split
the sea from the sky &
a serpent coiled around her
laid a dove's egg
& it
hatched & every-
thing
was born, including
us.

Kind of
stupid.

Without Wine Part 2

gone vinous hours
irritable bed scratch
blunted days
losing sight
wounding liver
emotional snap
vomiting on the clock
blind night march
receipts depleting balance

tea, time, poetry's wine
sweet, canned fruits, chopped
apples & pantry prunes
salad is wine
moist, dunked cookie

Without Wine Part 3

Oh WI
w/o wine
the streets are empty
yr huddled in bars.
W/o wine
no more witness
to dysfunctional liquor store transactions.
WI's w/o wine anyway!
Beer to Ear to Belly to Vomit to Deep
Fried Cheese, Meats, to
who's crying at the bar?
Who's going to fight? Fight!
Who's screaming? Who's playing w/ fire?
Who fell flat over backwards?
Is he bleeding
from the back of his head?
Can I take a hit?
Who has pills? Who wants pills?
Sex walked.
Would anyone like a glass of water?
Oh no, not tap water.
I'm vegan eating cheese curds
isn't that funny?
Everyone took their 1st sip of beer
as I sat w/ wine, witness.
Was that really wine? $10 a cheap one?
Are we headed out?
You never leave?
You were drunk when I came in?
You're my buddy. I don't understand
a single word you're saying.

You're sexy tonight. Sexy top. Phone.
Phone. Phone. Phone. Phone. Phone.
"Look at you's, all on yr phone,"
the bartender said.
Wanna shot? Have a shot.
Let's do shots! Shots!
Please don't drive. "I know what I'm doing."
Please don't drive. Arrested.
That picked up from jail Sunday morning.
That hungover in pew.
That drink w/ brunch!
He wrapped his car around a tree.
He killed one of his buddies.
She was flung 100 feet from the train.
I said awful things about eating babies.
W/o wine
he just slunk down & died.

Without Wine Part 4

W/o wine
I'm hydrated.
Air is my wine
take a deep breath.
The expression of drunkenness
is that everything is already drunk:

> birds in air
> new leaves in rain
> acrobatic squirrels
> flowers w/ color
> soil blotto at flood level
> galaxies swirling w/ tails of light

& yr just upright, drunk on yrself
not yr ego
drunk to drunk
meeting in streets
meeting in meeting
meeting at the show
everyone you meet: the cashier
waitress, anyone
in one wounded nation
believing its own gossip
sure of its beliefs
duped into division.
W/o wine
attention, follow-through & post.
W/o wine
you can pull the root
& plant yr own garden.

W/o wine, perhaps
you can have a glass!
No wine is wine
w/ or w/o wine.
It's not that I can't control it.
It's just I can't control the uncontrollable part!
The uncontrollable part is completely out of control!
Anger! Drink.
Friday night! Drink.
Weekend! Drink.
Party! Drink.
Holiday! Drink.
Summer! Drink.
Winter! Drink.
Let's get together! Drink.
& then I'm crawling out of my work week
having a drink.
Painting! Drink.
Relax. Drink.

Sparkling water, caffeinated drinks
tissues wet
save a few thousand bucks for a single drink
for good times with word pronunciation
complete sentences & projects
DO SOMETHING
w/o a loud mouth
BE LOUD w/o dirty mouth
take a hike, see a movie
got to a show, visit
friends, family, w/o wine
recluse w/o wine
do time w/o wine
one more time w/o wine
wet lips w/o wine

it's fine w/o wine
sunshine w/o wine
THE END w/o wine

w/o wine
THE END

Market Day Song

Market Day, Market Morning
Drank last night? That's no problem.
No need to brew coffee or make breakfast
just shower & dress & get your Market stuff.

Get your coffee & have a pastry.
Buy fresh food from local farmers.
The food won't go bad for weeks & weeks
& it tastes good unlike corporate junk.

Pain & Death Song

Does the consciousness light
go off when you die?
Oh why? Oh why?

Are you out like a light
when you die? When you die?
Good-bye? Good-bye?

Does pain depend
on living 'fore end?
The sky. The sky.

Would it all go away
buried to stay
today? Today?

I hope that it does
pain is worse when it comes.
Someday. Someday.

What is the end of this song?
Of its life? Of its tongue?
It's wrong? It's wrong?

Fart Poem

chickpeas are beans
    beans are seeds
seeds are the contents of fruit

Beans, beans the magical fruit
the more you eat the more you toot!

oligosaccharides
undigested through stomach, small intestine
oligosaccharides
for bacteria in the large intestine
oligosaccharides
break down in the gut

raffinose is an oligosaccharide, a saccharide polymer
a trisaccharide (galactose, glucose & fructose)
is a few sugars
a carbohydrate, synonym saccharide
raffinose $C_{18}H_{32}O_{16}$ for bacteria in the large intestine
raffinose breaks down in the gut

emissions from ass (He tore the fabric of spacetime!)
N, O, H, CO_2, methane (odorless)
99% of fart
hydrogen sulfide (smelly) H_2S
1% of fart
all people fart
France (péter), Fiji, Fuji, Fresno
Fido farts (reeks)
meat farts (reek)
eggs & fishy farts

bacteria farts inside
we fart their farts
who do we fart inside of?

4,000 years ago they joked about farts
ask a flatologist
a Norseman "breaks wind"
cows & cockroaches explode (boric acid)
the flautas eating flatus flautist performed in Jethro Tull

Scene from a Birthday

On my birthday
I was sitting on concrete steps
outside Milton High School
in the back by the pool
waiting for a nephew to come out
on the phone with Dad.
I said, "My doctor said
the CDC recommends 1 alcoholic drink a day."
Dad replied, "When Grandpa Sal was a younger man
he drank a bottle of port wine
& 12 beers a day.
When he got older, he cut back
& stopped drinking the wine.
When his teeth got bad
he started drinking his beer warm."
F. Scott Fitzgerald drank
40 beers a day?
I'm thinking
no liquor, forget the beer
drink red
spritz or don't, don't
finish the bottle alone.

Dad went on to say, "I swear to God
his bladder was the size of a football
sticking out of his stomach."
Prostate cancer wouldn't allow him to piss.
F. Scott died when he was 44.
Dolores O'Riordan, 47, drowned drunk
in a bathtub.
I'm 48. The neph, Gavin, came out

& a strange dog jumped into our car.
Gavin grabbed the dog tag on the collar
the dog's foreign face right up against his.
"Is this our dog?" I asked from the passenger seat
Mom in back, brother investigating outside.
"No!"
Gavin spotted similar dogs across the lot
& ran towards them
commanding our new dog to follow.
The dogs in the distance
a matching shaggy white & gray
bobbed & frolicked by their master
a man in a dark coat.
Our dog joined them
& Gavin ran back & got in.

Golden-crowned Kinglet

It was Mom's idea
to walk at Lake Kegonsa.
We parked at the far end
by the boat landing.
The water was dark gray
whitecapped.
It was so windy
we had to cut into the woods.
We drove
to the other end of the park
near the entrance
& walked into a deep woods loop.
Few buds, green, flowers.
It was about to rain.
Mom stopped
to look at some little birds.
They were twitching about
on lower branches
& the ground. Some
smaller than others.
They were mostly gray
with a brilliant yellow-orange stripe
up their forehead. They made
the few chickadees about
seem built, robust.
A few raindrops
pelted the dead leaves
so we got going
wondering
what kind of bird
it was.

Morning Cooper's Hawk

Raspy squawks out my morning window
        I thought it might be about a hawk.
Murder of crows hunched in green leaf branches
        staring at the bird
who eases into a dive silently
        at a crow
back up
        to a branch
dives again
        & again

easy as a skateboarder
        up a giant half-pipe
& down
        before tricks.

The Eastern Parson Spider

furry black with plasticky, dark sepia legs
        cravat across its back
perhaps the fastest spider in the north woods
        moving many times its length per second
females bigger than the males.

After it hunted in my bathroom for a couple of days
        creeping in under the bathroom door
leg by leg
        I saw a silverfish
on the other side of the apartment
           far from the toilet
probably horrified –
        I threw it outside.

1st cold day, 1st cold nights
        then 1st snow
spiders come.

The Old Man with the Cane

Day before Mother's Day walk
in the blossoming UW Arboretum
turkeys, gray catbirds, sandhill crane
Mom, brother, 2 nephews & I –
aging woman, bright & concerned asked
"Would you help my husband stand up?"
Eldest nephew wrapped his arms
around the old man's chest
man's hand heavy on the cane
legs wobbling fiercely – no go.
Brother & I walked with the woman
in search of a wheelchair; Mom & nephs
waited with the old man on the bench
under the tree.
"This never happened before,"
the woman said.
No wheelchair, a young man called a ranger.
In the meantime
we eyed the old man from a distance
as he fidgeted, turning left & right
attempting
to find footing &
rise.
No go. He fell back
his head against
the tree. "Maybe he's resting,"
I suggested.
Brother ran over
man raised his arm
to sit back up.

That ashen
blue-eyed man
looked me right in the eye.

What a beautiful
place
what a beautiful
wife
what a beautiful
day

to die.

Without Much Money *no puedes tener cosas bonitas*

W/o much money
you can't have nice things.
It was a miracle
    the washing machine worked
but the good dryer's coin slot was jammed.
Que lastima.
The apartment itself
    sucks.
No tengo ni coche ni mujer.
No puedo hablar frances o español
    con fluidez
a pesar de todo mi tiempo libre.
No puedo salir de la ciudad.
No puedo ver cosas bonitas!
No puedo tener cosas bonitas.
Sin mucho dinero
no puedes tener cosas bonitas.

6 Commercials

Advertisements for the following 6 products during a Super Bowl commercial break – Green Bay Packers vs Pittsburg Steelers, Feb 2011 – for Andy Gricevich

Chips
Cars
Pop
Halftime show
Pop
Chips

Portrait of Ron Czerwien

I saw him
from across the street
beautiful day
walking his Australian terrier
leash long held tight
into the parking garage
of Trader Joe's
wearing jeans & a
baseball cap over his
glasses & plaid
shirt – I imagined
he wanted to be holding
in his other hand
an umbrella.

White Poetry Chicks

I'm obsessed
with Anne Waldman
& Adrienne Rich – rhizome
& wreck – haunted by
Plath (in a classroom).

matriarchy, patriarchy, fraternity
hegemony, hickory, *boo!*

Chicks, dig, dig, d-i-g dig, dig metaphors

Boots – *for Sinéad O'Connor*

curious about this singer
    I hated in college
video in heavy rotation
    bald woman, long black coat
walking, walking
    gray statues, frost (Parc de Saint-Cloud)
I put on a greatest hits CD
    in my mother's garden
a petite, pink side room
    John I Love You, attention
the most beautiful song I'd ever heard
    Universal Mother
Throw Down Your Arms
    vam-pi-re
I thought of you
    hanging out with a bruiser
her vodka bottle up
    then your passing
no more boots

Visiting Dad in the ICU

I was directed to the right room
in the ICU
by his attendant. I didn't recognize
that head
in a sea of white sheets
with a storm of tubes & electronics
raining into it – I
walked out & asked the young woman
if it was Mr.
Stolte.

I began to recognize him.
Mouth open, eyes closed
he looked like a mummy
younger.

I sat awhile
as the attendant
changed drips &
worked with tubes on his
arms & legs.
Another attendant
came in & did something, looking @
one of the screens.
A doctor in blue asked in the doorway
if everything was alright.

I watched his brain scan
from left to right
changing a little after each
pass. His stomach twitched –

I thought that was a good sign.
His face, sedated
was absolutely
still.

He didn't make it.

Visiting Dad in the ICU the Day After His Accident the Day Before His Death

I sld've known he was dead
when I saw him in the ICU
      he looked like a mummy
eyes never open.

But his stomach twitched!
I thought he thought
      hamburger
I thought
      pizza.

I thought he'd be
fine.

I thought his stomach twitch
was a good sign.

Eyes Closed Repose

When Dad got dead
they put him in a sled.
No thoughts, snow, where to go.

What did he care?
He wasn't there.

Thumbs & Plum

Bigger than a berry
more like a plum
my dad had an aneurysm
tore an inch & a ½ long.
My dad had thumbs.

Gave each other a hug
damn plum.

Sure

No, Wanda
to live is to *bike*.

coffee morning
orgasm night

Write it
paint

someday you
ain't.

The 12 WI Months

SEP   Crash
OCT   Burn
NOV   Smoke
DEC   Dark

JAN   New
FEB   Light
MAR   Wind
APR   Rain
MAY   Spring
JUNE   Summer
JULY   Hot

AUG   Perfect

Eken Park – MAY 2024

An evening bike ride
      through the neighborhood

Branch down
      in the street
after a brief, severe storm.
      Police SUV blocks a lane
yellow DO NOT CROSS tape
      up the street, flashing red & blue overheads.
Brass, drum kit, band in the park shelter
      español!
Allium, columbine, bleeding heart
      drip rain late sun.
I found a vinyl record
      dusty wet in curb junk
but ok – I'll spin it tonight.
      Little libraries, boxes of books & food
for the street
      furniture, electronics.

South Dakota governor banned
      from tribal lands;
you get the Indians against you
      that's bad.

MON WALK

Whomp! Red-winged blackbird
      boxed my ears
back of my neck
      Olbrich Botanical Gardens;

shooting stars dominated
        Governor Nelson State Park.

DREAM

A coworker
        I'm interested in
gave me cookies –
        chocolate chip
w/ pepperoni & ham.

DREAM

President Joe Biden
        lay his shaky hand
on my shoulder, to steady himself.

Poynette woods full of Jack-in-the-pulpit
        invasive garlic mustard.

MAY yard sales – I sorted a tote
        of musty vinyl for a kid
Grandmother departed (10 years ago!)
        estate sale
I bought 3, 6 VHS.

Brown paper grocery bag
        painters, poets
yr work will end up in it
        me summer '98
David-Baptiste Chirot June 2021
        ton of work, no fun
that end up sum.
        (I wld've liked
some of DBC's VHS tapes

   like the Sex Pistols' **Filth
& Fury**.)

MON WALK

Rain coming – Korth Park
   W side of Rock Lake, Lake Mills
parking lot – walking with Mom
   to the trail head, woman
from SUV says, "The forest
   is full of phlox. It's everywhere. It's beautiful."
I approached the driver
   to inform her of dame's rocket
but Mom walked on. I followed.
   "I was going to tell her about
dame's rocket," I said. Mom said
   "We didn't need to spoil her day."
Glacial dip in the woods, mosquitos
   "It's everywhere, alright," I said.
Mom laughed.

We were able
   to take a 2nd walk
@ Olbrich Gardens
   on our way back – there
was stout, woodland phlox there.

Phlox is native, 5-petal flower;
   dame's rocket is invasive
4-petals.

Evening tornado warning – brief strong winds
   trees down all over the city
power outages. I figured out
   the name of a flower –

white campion.

In MAY
      landlords turn off the heat;
cold nights
      bath towels won't dry.

Texting a former resident
      the youngest person to move in
to the old folks' apartments
      pneumonia for 8 weeks
4, 5 & 6 ribs cracked, stacked
      up under her L armpit
from coughing.

Memorial Day weekend
      SAT morning bike out
for vegetables & wine –
      now to bike out
to see some wildflowers?

Bike back
      to the estate sale
no VHS – "We weren't
      supposed to put those out,"
the kid said. (I'd give
      my tapes back, but
they were only concerned about
      Teenage Mutant Ninja Turtles.)
I looked down – 2nd tote
      of vinyl. "More vinyl?"
I said. Good condition. Rock.
      I flipped through, grabbed 10
& got the hell out of there
      before someone came along & said

how valuable they are.
    1 to sell, 4 to gift
5 to keep. $1 each.

SUN – rain too heavy
    to bike out.
Rode to the grocery store anyway
    & collected some wildflowers
for a bouquet
    on the rainy ride home.

Spiderwort Pheasant Branch
    Hogweed Cherokee Marsh

Yellow golden Alexanders
    confused with
wild parsnip
    which have flat, compound umbels
phototoxic sap which blisters the skin
    & comes out a little later.

Rain. Biking in the rain.
Riding in the rain.
At home in the rain.
Puddle in my storage unit.

"Ach-chu!" HR representative sneezes
    caught in the afternoon
        monsoon.

Haiku

I celebrated New Year's
        by lifting my head from the pillow
to hear 1 firework.

                Slush, snow
                        April crow looks down –
                double lanes traveling east, west.

Charred tip of an incense stick
        behind the toilet base
not my long time no see silverfish.

                Biking back
                      croaking frogs –
                How many Springs?

Like a childish or brute painting
        indigo up
over low green.

                Hawk jumped the busy street fence
                      stared back through it –
                dead duck in roadside gravel.

Enduring my neighbor practicing guitar
    I have to close the windows
when the amateur brass band practices.

           Unemployed, no breakfast, no lunch
                no wine yet
        working on poems.

Evening walk – 1st fireflies
    I really have been
drinking less.

           Drinking water at night
               fresh as
         afternoon wine.

No wine for 3 days –
    tomorrow a toast
to 3 days.

           Cars pass my window
                quick – butterflies
         too.

Click click click claws on concrete
        across snout straight
morning night bike coyote.

                White fluff cottonwood seeds
                      float –
                pop stars.

Long way
        from the notebook
to the book.

                Barefoot, shitting, anything
                      the apt. isn't big enough –
                scutigera coleoptrata.

Notes

Senti is an Italian verb form of *sentire* meaning "to hear", "to feel" or "to listen."

The Man with Tubes Up His Nose – This poem has nothing to do with *Tubes* by Donald Hall. The poem begins: "Up, down, good, bad," said/ the man with tubes/ up his nose, "there's lots/ of variety …"

Allen Ginsberg was deported from Cuba then Czechoslovakia in 1965, for "outspokenness."

Aunt Carrie – 1960-2023, died of lung cancer

Gerunds end in "ing". How much do you ski when you ski?

Things Nadine Said – written DEC 20, 2013

Nadine is Dead Song – written DEC 10, 2013

At the Reading – for Tony Robinson 1995-2015

Table for One – Despite a shocking amount of information online, including years of jail time for assaulting a 9-year-old in a parking lot & frequent mugshots, I choose to let this individual remain anonymous. Photos of her were put up by the front door with a note telling residents to report this individual to the police on sight.

Portrait of Chris Cornell – 1964-2017, Seattle singer, songwriter

Without Wine Parts 2-4 – *W/o Wine* is in **Sentimental Slop & Haiku**, 2021

Market Day! Song – written Saturday NOV 9, 2013

Andy Gricevich – Madison WI poet, forager

Ron Czerwien – Madison WI poet, owner of Avol's Books, LLC

White Poetry Chicks – end lyric by Sparks, an L.A. band consisting of the Mael brothers, debut album 1972

Boots – for Sinéad O'Connor, 1966-2023, Irish singer, songwriter, activist

Leonard William Stolte – 1955-2023, author's father

Wanda Colman – L.A. Poet, NOV 1946-NOV 2013

The 12 WI Months – Due to climate change, WI is warmer – these categories don't quite fit anymore. For example, this year's AUG was Hot & SEP was Perfect.

Eken Park – May 2024 – Neighborhood in East Madison WI, approximately equidistant from the state capitol to the SW & the interstate to the NE.

David-Baptiste Chirot – 1953-2021, longtime Milwaukee poet/ artist, maker of rubBEings

www.ingramcontent.com/pod-product-compliance
Lightning Source LLC
Chambersburg PA
CBHW031645040426
42453CB00006B/218